29.95

MW00700345

Brush with Life
Writing Chinese words of virtue and celebration

（筆墨緣）

Text by Martha Dahlen 杜雅文 and Grace Ho 何陳賽蘭
Calligraphy of title and dedication by Grace Ho 何陳賽蘭,
of words and phrases by Ho Siu Kei 何兆基

Designed and printed by C A Design, Hong Kong

Distributed in Asia by
United Century Book Services Ltd.
Unit 504, Westlands Centre
20 Westlands Road
Quarry Bay, Hong Kong

ISBN 962-7502-58-8

願我們的真善美
活於字裏行間

In writing, may our innermost truth, kindness, and beauty

live within the words and between the lines

Brush with Life
Writing Chinese words of virtue and celebration

I. INTRODUCTION

This book presents some of the most common single words and four-character phrases that the Chinese use for decoration, celebration, and inspiration. It is meant for those who would like to write characters themselves with brush and ink, but who are not necessarily fluent in Chinese. This is both possible and desirable. As with the other arts, calligraphy offers beginner and expert equal opportunity to express, to explore and to create. In addition, the very act of writing has the power to calm the mind and spirit. Through careful attention and intention, anyone can benefit from writing even a few characters.

EVERY DAY, EVERYWHERE

Today, as has been true for centuries, the Chinese commonly use the characters of their language as decoration. Framed calligraphy hangs on the walls of restaurants, stores, and businesses as well as homes, offices, and art galleries. The characters for Good Fortune and Double Happiness (Marital Bliss) appear as motifs on fabric, porcelain, furniture, jewelry, even candy wrappers. Dramatic gold characters top off calendars. In watching Chinese films, of any genre and any era, you will invariably catch a glimpse of calligraphy displayed somewhere.

This differs distinctly from the Western use of their language, where most of the words we see are logos or trademarks. Why? One might argue that this divergence is logical, given the pictographic nature of the Chinese characters and the remarkably expressive, capabilities of their writing implement, the brush. Such writing communicates not only concepts but also emotions, speaking directly to deep parts of our human nature. For whatever reasons, calligraphic works are universally admired, and the practice of calligraphy is revered as an exercise in self-development. To write well requires concentration, discipline, and skill; it represents long, attentive, patient practice. To the extent that each stroke reveals and expresses something fundamental about the writer, it can inspire and uplift the reader.

Beyond that, one must also note the subtle wisdom in this Chinese habit, which is remarkably similar to the modern practice of using "affirmations". To achieve your best it makes sense to set up your environment to inspire and instruct as well as to evoke feelings of virtue and pleasure. This is what the Chinese do by displaying calligraphy.

THE FREQUENT FOUR

A second unusual feature of the Chinese language is the rich repertoire of four-character phrases that are used to celebrate virtually every special occasion in a human life. These phrases cover a spectrum of common aspirations, hopes, and desires, using rich images and expressing hearty confidence. The four-character pattern seems to derive from ancient Chinese classical literature. Snappy, concise, and rhythmic, it survives—and thrives—today in a plethora of proverbs and modern slogans, as well as these holiday expressions and salutations.

IMAGE AS EXPRESSION

Before starting to write, some understanding

of what makes the Chinese language and the Chinese brush particularly expressive may help you both write better and more thoroughly appreciate Chinese calligraphy you see.

Each character in the Chinese language is composed of one or more fundamental elements that are called "radicals". There are more than 200 radicals, of which many look like what they mean. For example, this is the wood radical: 木 (like a tree); the mouth radical: 口; and this is the word for the chirping of birds (zao): 噪. This is the sun radical: 日; the moon radical: 月 and the word for bright is (ming): 明. So a Chinese character is composed of radicals in the way that an English word is composed of letters, but the radicals may not be arranged linearly in the character, and the component radicals have meaning themselves, aside from or in addition to the meaning of the overall character. (Some component radicals indicate

pronunciation rather than meaning; with over 5000 characters, the situation is complex and will not be covered further here.) In learning to recognize characters, look for the radicals; in writing, think of them as subunits within the character as a whole. In all situations, appreciate that reading these pictographic words probably involves more of the creative, imaginative right brain than reading a line of Western letters.

Secondly, Chinese grammar is far less complex and specific than English, with the result that much more of the meaning is left up to the reader. In translating Chinese into English, one must usually supply conjunctions and prepositions and assign grammatical function—according to your understanding. Interpretations vary, and complex concepts that can be represented by a few Chinese characters may need a long English story when translated. Hence, in reading Chinese (especially these four-character phrases), aim to develop concepts rather than to find the precise English equivalent, and simply allow that rich conceptual understanding to inform your strokes.

A third element that makes Chinese calligraphy particularly expressive are the tools of the art—carbon ink, absorbent paper, and a remarkably adept brush. With its round head and resilient bristles, a Chinese brush can move with equal facility in any direction, as well as toward or away from the paper. Like a dancer, it should move with rhythm and grace, producing dynamic lines, sharp edges, crisp dots, and bold curves, spontaneously, in dynamic proportion. The result is truly a work of art.

Good calligraphy gives the impression of life. Seasoned calligraphers maintain that anyone can distinguish good from bad, simply by looking. How? By reading the feeling. Open your senses to what you experience as you see it, imagine the brush as it must have swept across the page, examine the subtle variations that give the strokes dynamic tension... This kind of "reading" will not only develop your appreciation, but also improve your writing.

Now, prepare to try...

II. INSTRUCTIONS
EQUIPMENT

The **brush** must be round. Ideally, it should come to a very fine point, hold much ink, and be resilient (i.e. spring back to original shape after a stroke). Of the oriental brushes available, white hairs (e.g., sheep, goat) hold more ink but are less resilient, while brown hairs (e.g., wolf, boar) tend to be more resilient but hold less ink. Many beginners prefer the firmer, dark hairs, but choice is largely a matter of personal preference.

New brushes have glue holding the bristles in a conical shape. This should be washed out under running water, for about 80% of the length of the bristles. In use, ink will gradually soften the bristles all the way. This is essential because the upper part of the brush acts as a reservoir, feeding ink to the tip as the brush moves across the paper. When you finish writing, wash only excess ink out of the brush; no need to clean it perfectly. Shake to remove excess water (form the hairs into a point and replace the cap if you wish), then hang it to dry. Don't worry if the bristles become stiff; when you are ready to write again, soak the bristles in ink (not water) until they are softened.

As for the **ink**, traditionally, sticks of carbon (were) are ground on stone to produce ink as thick or thin as required. The grinding was itself considered meditative preparation for writing. Today, most calligraphers use bottled ink; India ink will also work. In use, it should have the consistency of thin cream.

Chinese writing supplies. Above, the traditional materials. Below, modern time-saving equivalents. Even a round Western watercolor brush and sketch-pad (upper right) can be used.

If too thin—strokes either look pale or swell (on Chinese paper)—then pour the ink out into a shallow dish, and let it thicken by evaporation. If too thick, add water.

As for **paper**, oriental papers are generally more absorbent and therefore more expressive than Western: this also makes them more difficult to work with! They come in a range of textures and qualities; experiment to find what suits you best. For practicing, unprinted newspaper can be used. For final pieces, Chinese stationery stores often sell decorative cards and papers (red, red with gold flecks; etc.) specifically for calligraphy.

In addition, you need a piece of **wool cloth** or felt to cover the table on which you will work. The cloth provides a firm, resilient, only slightly absorbent surface that will help paper, brush and ink work together.

TECHNIQUE

Hand position. Hold the brush so that it is perpendicular to the paper. Arrange your fingers as shown in the photographs, with thumb on one side and the fingers spread on the other. Note the wrist angle.

Arm position. While there is only one hand position, arm position varies according to the size of characters you are writing. Ordinarily, the writing arm rests lightly on the paper while the other hand anchors the paper—as in writing Western letters. When writing very small characters, you may rest your writing arm on the other hand, as pictured. In writing large characters, hold the forearm above and parallel to the paper (also pictured).

Movement. In all cases, the thumb and first finger hold and move the brush while the other fingers merely support and guide. Keep your back upright; breathe evenly. Generate movement from the shoulder (ideally, from the abdomen where vital energy is stored), not from the fingers. As you write, move the paper—not your hand—in order to maintain the writing hand in the same position relative to the body (i.e., in front of the side of the chest).

Making strokes. Observe the models carefully, and try to recreate the nuances of thick and thin as well as the proportional relationships of the strokes.

For those new to the Chinese brush, we offer these pointers:

1. As a **warm-up exercise**, make figure 8's. One on top of another, up, down, left, right, stretching in each direction. Then practice individual strokes.

2. **Squared ends**. As illustrated, any blunt start or end of a stroke involves a slight reverse movement of the brush. This makes the ends slightly thicker—like the ends of a bone or the anchor points of a stretched cord.

When writing very small characters, you may rest your writing arm on the other hand.

Holding the brush for writing large characters. Note that the forearm is held above and parallel to the paper.

3. **Tapered or pointed ends**. These are made by pulling the brush in the direction of the point, pressing, then lifting as you reach the end.

4. **Dots** are made with a circular or oval motion of the brush tip, with some spreading of the brush in the middle.

5. In writing **boxes**, the top and right side are considered a single stroke. Pull the brush to the right, pause at the corner, then pull the brush downward.

6. After gaining some familiarity with individual strokes, try **words**. Classic texts particularly recommend writing the

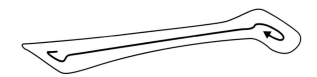

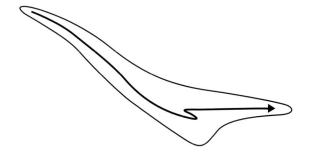

Stroke order for the common practice word 'yong', meaning eternal.

character *yong* (meaning 'eternal')
to develop skill.

7. Especially try words in **different styles**.
   You may find that you can write one style
   better than another. Enjoy it!

Stroke order. The order in which the strokes
are made subtly affects the appearance of the
final character as each stroke leaves the hairs
of the brush in a particular arrangement, and
puts the hand in a particular position, relative
to the beginning of the next stroke. In general,
the order is: ***top to bottom — left to right —
outside to inside.***

These rules are most useful for writing the
standard script. For seal script, there is
controversy, even among calligraphers, and
somewhat less importance because the strokes
are so uniform. For the running and grass
scripts, order is critical but highly personal;
one must examine the model to discern the
path of the brush for copying and learning
each character.

In this book, we provide the stroke order and
brush stroke path for the larger characters only.
With practice from these models you will
develop an instinct as to how to write
any character. If you feel you need more
explicit instructions, please consult a Chinese
textbook.

CALLIGRAPHIC STYLES
In this book you will find each character or
phrase written in one or more of the five
fundamental styles of Chinese calligraphy,
as described below.

Zhuan shu *(Seal script, 篆書)* – The most
ancient and primitive form, this style
originated in the Qin Dynasty when the
premier at the time, Li Si, devised a single
writing system that became the first uniform
script for the Han people. It is a simple
regular style; each stroke is of uniform width
and has rounded ends; verticals and
horizontals tend to be strictly thus. Its beauty
derives from evenness and the balance of
space and line.

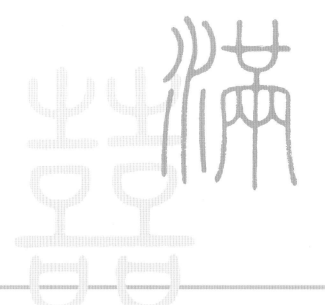

Zhuan Shu   *Li Shu*   *Kai Shu*

Li shu *(Clerical script, 隸書)* – This style was developed later than the seal script and is close to the standard script. Strokes are straight and broad, with strong crisp starts and finishes. Note that the characters are somewhat compressed horizontally, hence giving a sense of weight and solidity.

Kai shu *(Standard script, 楷書)* – Less formal than clerical script, this became the standard during the Jin Dynasty (c. 300 AD). Strokes vary in weight, but all are crisply executed, with precision and harmony. This is the foundation script for learning calligraphy; writing the more loose scripts (running and grass) well depends on mastery of original character structure as represented by *kai shu*. At the same time, this is also the most difficult script to master because its beauty derives from subtle aspects of brushwork and stroke geometry. Beginners should be patient and persevere; occasionally writing the other styles may give relief and encouragement.

Xing shu *(Running script, 行書)* – This script was also developed around 300 AD. Note that strokes within the character tend to be connected in a "running" movement of the brush. The strokes are softer, giving the piece of writing a more poetic appearance. (N.B. Observe that with this, as with standard and grass scripts, "horizontal" lines actually slant slightly upward giving a dynamic lift to the writing.)

Cao Shu *(Grass script, 草書)* – Also developed around 300 AD, this is the most fluid, brief and simplified form of writing. Not only are the strokes of individual characters simplified and connected, but also the words themselves are often linked, and the spatial arrangement of these characters in a text is less rigid. The freedom of movement and composition makes this one of the most popular styles of calligraphy—as well as one of the hardest to read because the brushwork is highly personal.

Xing Shu   *Cao Shu*

III. THE WRITING MODELS

The models in this book (beginning on page 22) fall into three categories: words and phrases used to celebrate Chinese New Year; words and phrases used to celebrate the important occasions of a lifetime; and a section of virtues. For the phrases, on the left with the large character, you will find an overall translation. On the right you will find the Pinyin pronunciations and a word-by-word translation—illustrating the grammatical difference between English and Chinese.

IV. TEMPLATES

Pages 128 and 129 are blank practice grids, just like the grids on which the models are presented. Copying characters on to grid-paper is a time-honored method for learning Chinese! After the grids come traditional templates for producing lucky banners.

V. FINAL WORDS

We have supplied enough instruction so that you can begin writing with brush and ink, correctly and confidently. We have tried to supply models that will intrigue and inspire you. All that is missing, perhaps, are a few final words of encouragement. Using a brush requires discipline, concentrated attention, and repeated practice. You must learn to guide rather than control, to understand the nature of brush, ink and paper—as well as of your self. It is not easy! But it is definitely worthwhile. The very act of writing has the power to settle the spirit and focus the mind. Through exercise one learns lessons of harmony, beauty, and self-mastery that soon find expression in the shape, style and vigor both of your brushstrokes and of your life.

Now it is time to begin…. Have fun!

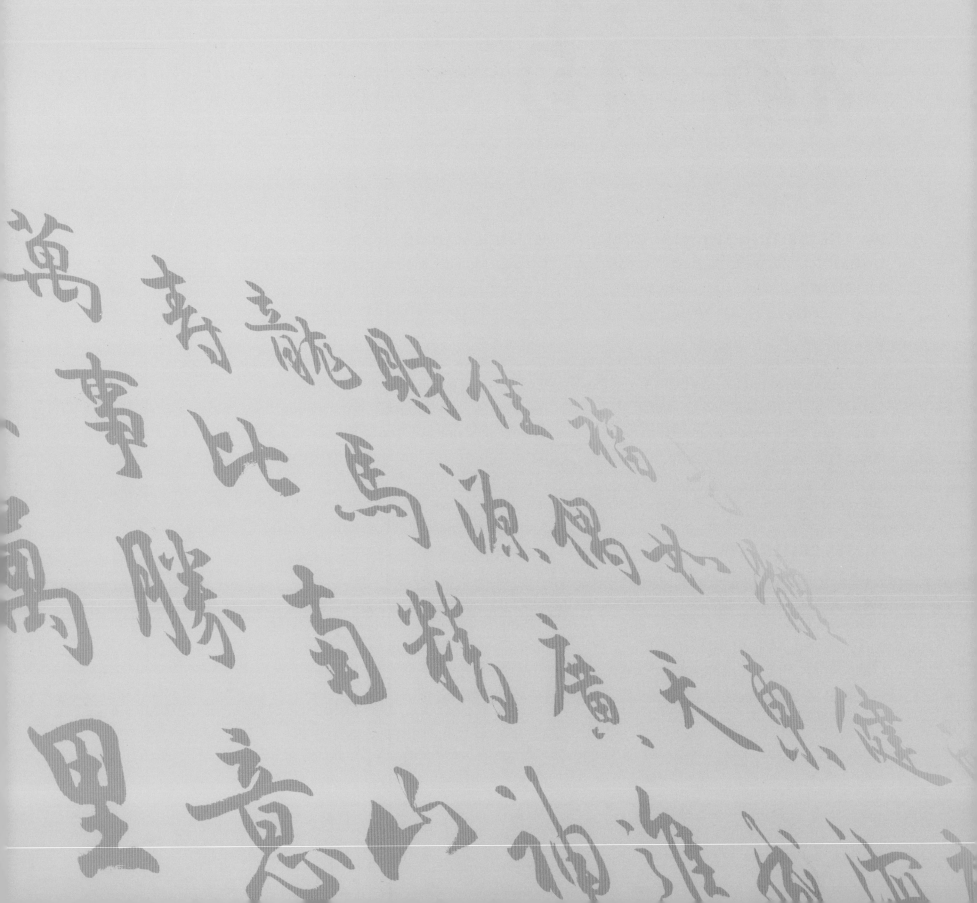

Model Characters & Phrases

Celebrating Chinese New Year

The New Year is by far the most significant, most widely and thoroughly celebrated of any holiday in China. The belief is strong that how you begin the year will influence your fortune throughout the coming months, just as how the soil is prepared influences the final harvest. Hence, as the New Year approaches, people pay off old debts, clean house, buy new clothes (particularly in red), prepare gifts for family and friends, cook auspicious foods, decorate their homes with blooming flowers, and hang red banners proclaiming their hopes for every sort of prosperity in the new year. It is customary for the entire family to gather for a meal on New Year's Eve, then welcome in the new year with firecrackers to scare away any unfriendly spirits or unlucky energy. Traditionally, business stops; people visit their families and rest, consciously preparing for the start of a new cycle.

Banners and posters are an indispensable part of Chinese New Year celebrations. They appear everywhere—in homes, offices, businesses, and stores. Common ones are printed in black on red paper; more elegant ones are written in gold on red paper. There is a glorious repertoire of phrases to choose from, or individuals may compose their own. In this way each person may express his personal aspirations, hopes and dreams for the new year, and set the stage for achieving them.

The following pages offer a selection of some of the most popular and colorful words and phrases for this all-important season.

(N.B. Traditionally, the Chinese follow a lunar calendar, in which the year begins with the new moon that falls sometime between mid-January and mid-February of the solar calendar. In addition, each year corresponds to one of 12 zodiac animals. New Year's days for the past 70 years are given on p.125, with calligraphic models of the corresponding animals on p.124.)

春 Chun

Spring

一 二 三 丰 夫
夫 春 春 春

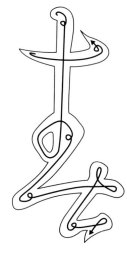

22

This word conveys all the connotations of the season itself: celebration and hope of renewal, the opportunity for a fresh start and the exhilaration of new energy. This character is often written large and put up starting 3–4 weeks before New Year's day. It may be hung upside down as a sign that spring will certainly arrive, as the Chinese character for 'upside down' (倒) sounds the same as the word for 'arrive' (到).

福 **Fu**

Good Fortune

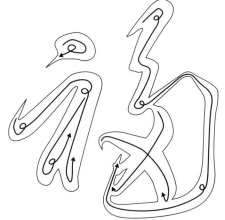

福 福
福 福

'Fu' is a happy character. It symbolizes heaven's blessing, manifest in all the good things in life; it exudes easy-going confidence that things will turn out right. Like 'Chun' (Spring), 'Fu' is often hung upside down during the New Year season, particularly at entrances. During the rest of the year, 'fu' appears as a design motif on all sorts of things from porcelain to fabric, from keyrings to calendars.

發 Fa

Expand & Develop

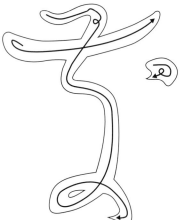

This character occurs in a huge number of compounds where it represents increase, expansion and development, for processes ranging from bread rising to wealth accumulating. At Chinese New Year in Hong Kong, "fa" is commonly seen and heard as part of 'Gung Hei Fat Choy!', which is the Cantonese pronunciation of 'Gong Xi Fa Cai' (see p.33); it is also displayed alone, particularly on calendars. Gamblers and businessmen especially like to manifest this characteristic.

滿 **Man**

Fullness, Fulfillment

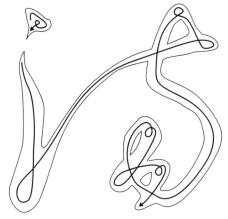

The usual translation of this character is "fullness", in the physical sense of having enough. The symmetry of the strokes, however, suggests a deeper concept in which balance and harmony generate not only fullness but also fulfillment. In the past, this character was pasted on the lid of the family's rice container symbolizing ample food throughout the coming year. Today, it is more commonly seen on refrigerators.

恭賀新禧

Congratulations and best wishes!

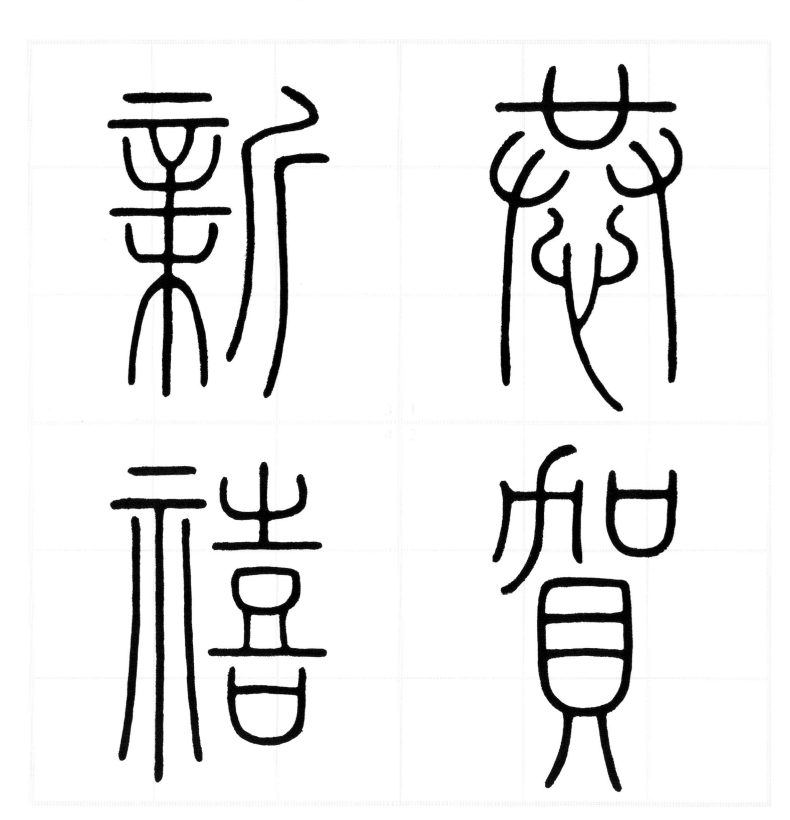

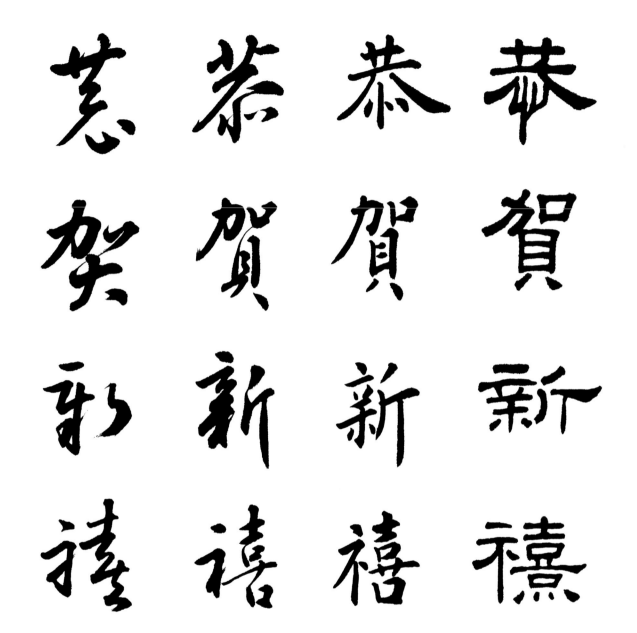

Gong He Xin Xi

(Respectful - congratulate - new - blessings)

This is probably the most common written greeting used during Chinese New Year. It appears on cards and banners, particularly in places of business. It is a more formal and less personal phrase used to greet clients in business, general acquaintances, and less close friends.

恭喜發財

Be happy and prosper!

Gong Xi Fa Cai

(Respectful - happy - generate - wealth)

In Hong Kong, this is probably the most commonly used New Year's phrase. There, the Cantonese use it as a lighthearted, friendly greeting, interpreting "cai" in a broad sense.

新年快樂

Happy New Year!

Xin Nian Kuai Le

(New - year - quick - happy)

This straightforward translation of the English is becoming increasingly common. It serves equally well for the solar New Year season, running up to January 1.

步步高陞

Step by step, moving up

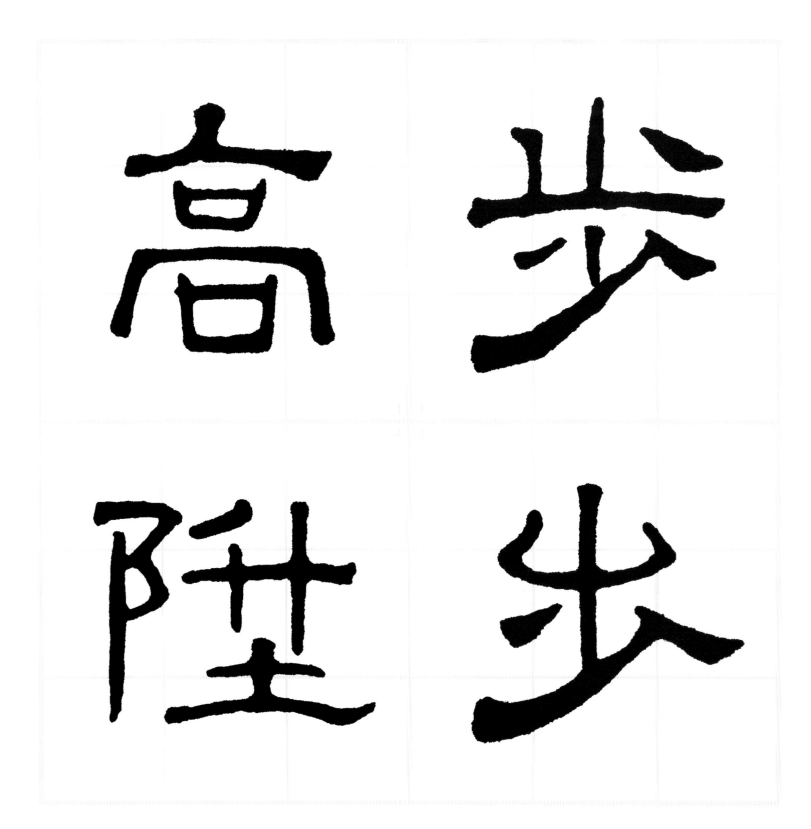

Bu Bu Gao Sheng

(Step - step - high - promote)

This phrase is used to encourage both children in their studies and young people in their careers, especially if the latter are climbing a corporate ladder.

財源廣進

Wealth coming from far and wide

Cai Yuan Guang Jin

(Wealth - source - broaden - enter)

The second character, 'yuan', is also the word for fountainhead, hence the image of wealth gushing like water from a spring. The fourth character, 'jin', is also a part of the common compound for progress ('jin bu' 進步); hence, the connotation of improvement as well as growth.

大吉大利

Big luck, big profit

大
吉
大

大
吉
大
利

大
吉
大
利

大
吉
大
利

Da Ji Da Li

(Big - luck - big - profit)

This simple phrase is popular for cards and banners. The entire phrase may be used, or either two-character compound ('Da Ji', or 'Da Li') alone.

花開富貴

Blooming flowers bring forth good fortune and honor

Hua Kai Fu Gui

(Flowers - open - wealth - esteemed, honorable)

The suggestion here is that wealth and status are a natural expression or display of inner virtue, just as a blooming flower naturally displays its latent beauty. The phrase is associated with wealthy people, but is equally appropriate for anyone who feels their life is blooming with richness .

滿堂富貴

Family gatherings bring forth good fortune and honor

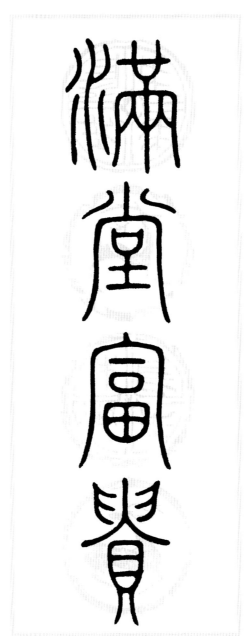

Man Tang Fu Gui

(Full - meeting hall - wealth - honorable)

The second character, 'tang', originally referred to the central courtyard of a Chinese extended family. The phrase attempts to capture the deep glow of warmth, contentment, pride and honor one feels when beloved sons, daughters, and grandchildren gather at home with their parents.

福祿壽全

Good Fortune, security, prestige and long life: All are yours

福　福　福　福
祿　祿　祿　祿
壽　壽　壽　壽
全　全　全　全

Fu Lu Shou Quan

(Fortune - official salary - longevity - altogether)

'Fu Lu Shou' represent all the good things in life. 'Fu' is good fortune (see pp.24–25); 'shou' means long life (see pp.66–67). The literal meaning of 'lu' refers to the setup in ancient China whereby a person who passed the official state examinations earned prestige as well as a government job for life. 'Fu Lu Shou' are often depicted as three jolly men, each bearing the symbols of his quality; they appear in paintings and as a group of statues near altars and shrines in traditional restaurants and businesses.

This phrase is also appropriate for birthdays.

福星拱照

Lucky stars honor and look after you

Fu Xing Gong Jiu

(Fortune - star - cup hands and bow - look after)

As in Western culture, men look to the heavens for blessing and good fortune. In addition, here, the third character suggests that your lucky stars also have great respect for you.

吉祥如意

Heaven grants your wishes

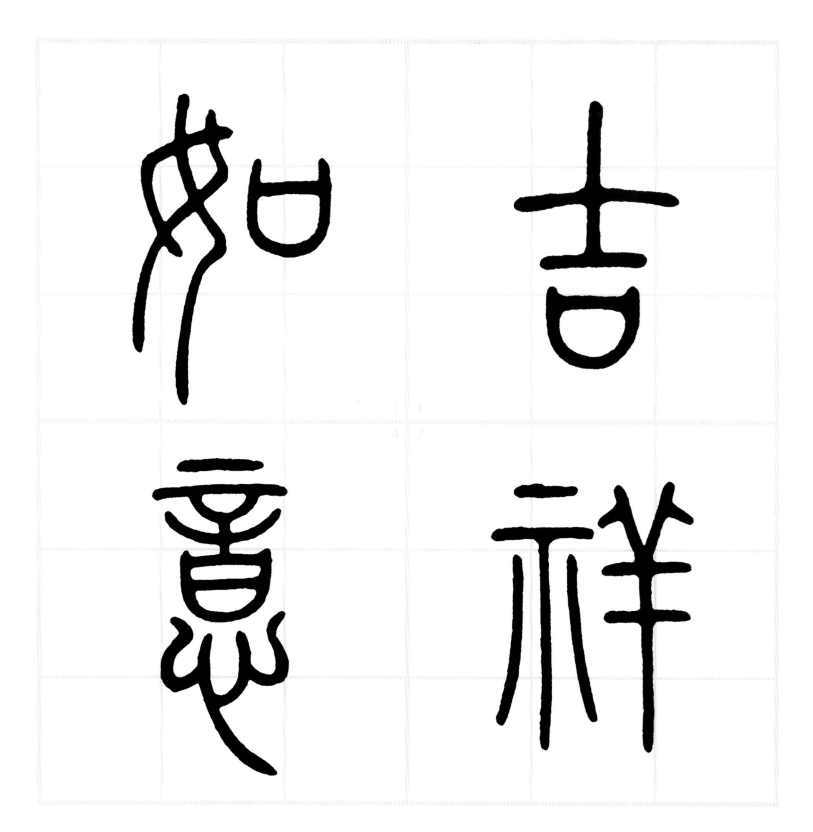

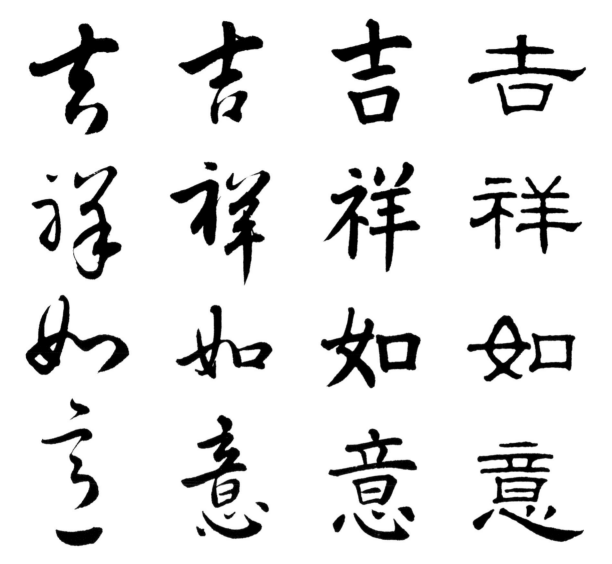

Ji Xiang Ru Yi

(Auspicious - auspicious - comparable to - intention)

This is a loosely constructed phrase composed of very common two-character phrases. That is, both 'Ji Xiang' and 'Ru Yi' are used alone; and when together, either may come first (i.e., in HK, 'Ru Yi Ji Xiang' while in Taiwan, 'Ji Xiang Ru Yi'). 'Ji Xiang' is most commonly translated as "lucky". It means blessed by heaven and implies that the things you want naturally come your way.

This phrase is appropriate at Chinese New Year or for birthdays, and is written vertically, horizontally, or in a circle or diamond shape.

龍馬精神

Spirit of dragon and horse:
Fly high! Charge ahead!

龍 龍 龍 龍
馬 馬 馬 馬
精 精 精 精
神 神 神 神

Long Ma Jing Shen

(Dragon - horse - essence, exquisite - spirit, soul)

This phrase expresses vigor and vitality. In Chinese lore, the dragon symbolizes heavenly greatness, while the horse represents earthly power, strength, and stamina. This phrase is popular among people whose work demands great energy, confidence, and fast decision-making, as well as among those who follow the horse races. It is particularly common during Years of the Dragon and Horse.

年年有餘

Year after year, surplus

Nian Nian You Yu

(Year - year - exist - surplus)

This is a simple wish for abundance and for the security which abundance brings, year after year.

The phrase has a counterpart in Chinese New Year cuisine. As the word for surplus (yu, 餘) sounds like the word for fish (yu, 魚), a whole fish is traditionally served at every New Year's celebration dinner, and it is important that some fish be left over. It is reported that in earlier days during lean years, farmers might serve a wooden fish to ensure that his hungry family would not eat all the "surplus".

平安 **Ping An**

Peace and Safety

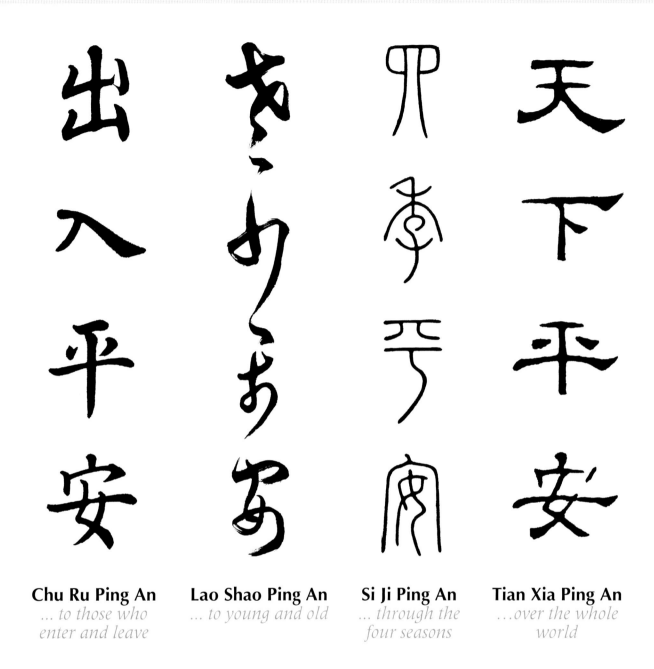

Chu Ru Ping An
... to those who enter and leave

Lao Shao Ping An
... to young and old

Si Ji Ping An
... through the four seasons

Tian Xia Ping An
...over the whole world

While both 'ping' and 'an' are individually translated as "peaceful", they have different connotations. 'Ping' can also mean even, level, flat; it implies, stability and expresses the tranquility of routine. 'An' is part of another expression meaning safety, hence it brings this sense to 'ping an'.

Four of the many four-character phrases using 'ping an' are given here. 'Chu Ru Ping An' is commonly written horizontally, and pasted above doorways. 'Lao Shao Ping An' is appropriate for households of more than one generation.

三陽開泰

A bold start ensures a smooth finish

San Yang Kai Tai

(Three - yang - opens - tranquility)

In this phrase, Triple Yang refers to an I Ching trigram that is composed entirely of yang lines. In Daoist philosophy, "yang" represents the masculine, active principle, bright, bold, and positive. But Yang at its extreme becomes yin; hence the third and fourth characters express this transformation into a smooth, tranquil playing out of whatever was begun.

萬事勝意

In every undertaking, success

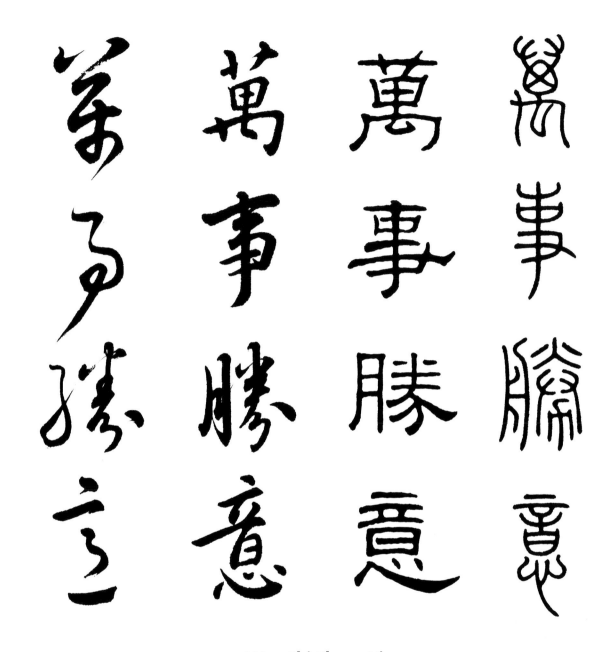

Wan Shi Sheng Yi

(Ten thousand - activity - victory, success - intention)

The first character of this phrase is poetically used to represent, myriad, uncountable objects. The final character suggests an inner desire or heartfelt intention. This phrase is used in banners and greetings during the Chinese New Year's season, and during the rest of the year when beginning a new project.

一團和氣

In unity, harmony and vitality

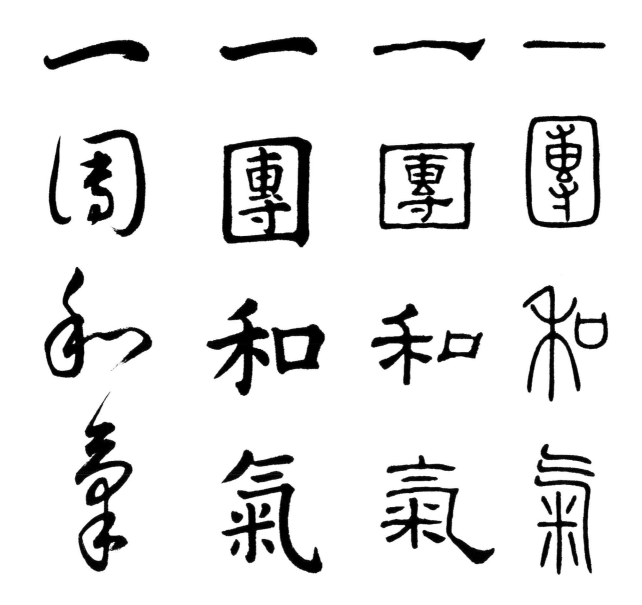

Yi Tuan He Qi

(One - unite; group - harmony, peace - vital energy)

The second word, 'tuan', with its boxlike form, is a true depiction of its meaning. At Chinese New Year, 'tuan' is part of an idiomatic phrase for family reunion, but the reference here could be to any group to which one belongs—from birth family, to company, to nation, to the whole human family. In any group, the dynamic synergy of harmony benefits all.

迎春接福

Welcome spring and receive good fortune

Ying Chun Jie Fu

(Welcome - spring - receive - fortune)

The first and third words, 'ying' and 'jie', are more commonly used together as a compound meaning greet. The arrangement of words emphasizes the welcoming and receiving of the blessings associated with the New Year.

Celebrating
Life's Milestones

As with New Year, the Chinese have a repertoire of words and four-character phrases to celebrate many of life's special events. The following pages present some of these celebratory words and slogans, beginning with those used for birthdays. In addition, many of the New Year's phrases are also used on these occasions—when the phrase fits, use it!

壽 **Shou**

Longevity

General Birthday. The calligraphy should be bold and vigorous, expressing the vitality that we all want to characterize a long life. You may also stretch the calligraphy out, from top to bottom, into a rectangle. This makes the character itself 'chang' or long, mimicking the meaning.

This character is appropriate for birthday cards, gifts and decorations for anyone, of any age. Stylized versions of it (as depicted on the page of the Table of Contents) are commonly used as decorative motifs on all manner of objects from furniture to fabric.

生辰快樂
Happy Birth-hour

Sheng Chen Kuai Le

(Give birth to - traditional Chinese hour - happy - joyful)

General Birthday. If the second character in the phrase above is replaced with the word for 'day' (re 日), then the phrase is exactly, 'Happy Birth-day'. The older, more traditional form as written here uses 'chen', a unit of time in ancient China. In those times, each day was divided into 12 segments, each of which was one 'chen', equivalent to two of our modern 60-minute hours. In addition, 'chen' names the Fifth Earthly Branch, a term in Daosim and geomancy. Hence, 'chen' is not only a more precise specification, but also an allusion to the heavenly blessings that derive from astrological configurations at one's moment of birth.

快高長大

Grow up quickly!

快高去大

快高長大

快高長大

快高長大

Kuai Gao Chang Da

(Fast - tall - long - big)

Child's Birthday. This phrase delights children, who naturally want to grow tall and strong as quickly as possible.

壽如松柏

Long life with honor and dignity

壽 壽 壽 壽
如 如 如 如
松 松 松 松
柏 柏 柏 柏

Shou Ru Song Bai

(Longevity - like - pine - cypress)

Older Person's Birthday. The pine and cypress are two classic symbols of long life, honor and dignity, in all the Chinese arts. Both are long-lived, noble, evergreen trees, hence fitting symbols for an elderly person on his/her birthday.

青春長駐

Youth and beauty lasting forever

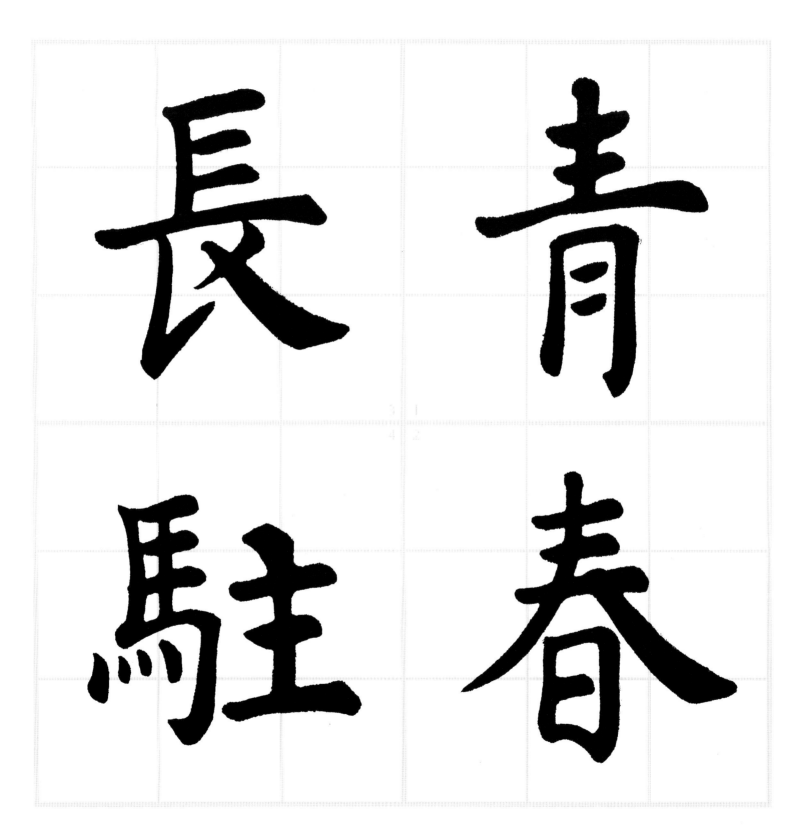

Qing Chun Chang Zhu

(Green, young - spring - long - halt)

Woman's Birthday. Here, simple words convey an exquisite thought. A more eloquent and complete translation might be, "May time stand still, preserving your youth and beauty like a fresh spring blossom forever."

萬壽無疆

Life without end

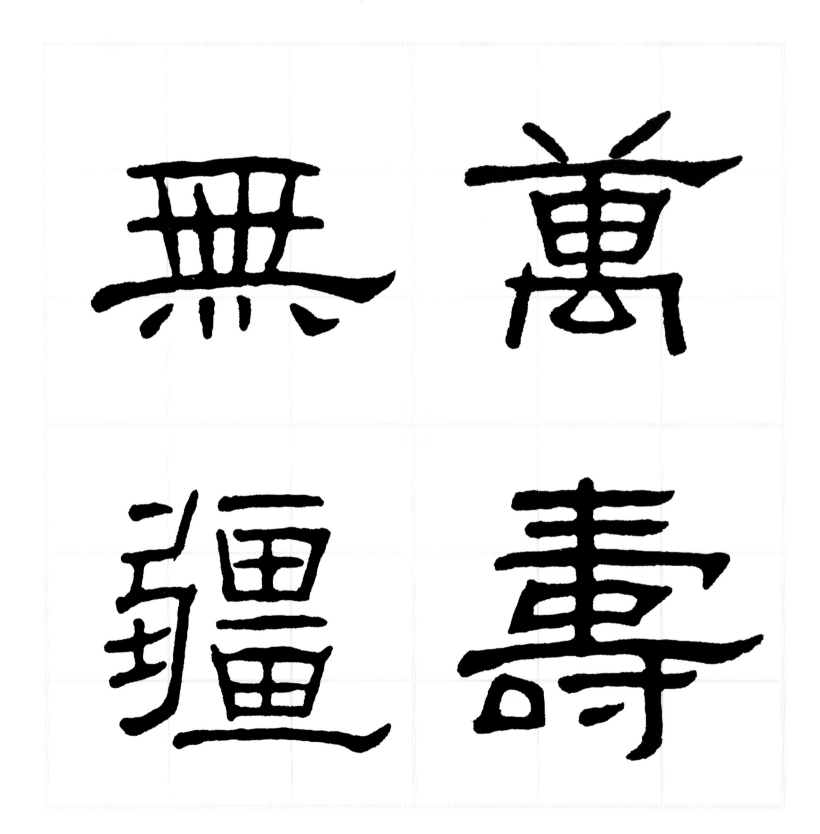

Wan Shou Wu Jiang

(Ten thousand - longevity - not - boundary)

Respected Person's Birthday. This phrase is both dramatic and formal, most appropriately used in written form for someone to whom you owe respect, for example, a leader, a teacher or master, a grandparent.

福如東海

Good fortune as bountiful as the deepest ocean

Fu Ru Dong Hai

(Good fortune - comparable to - east - sea)

General Birthday. Each of the phrases on page 78 and 79 can be used alone, or they can be used together as a couplet. As is ideal for Chinese couplets, each character in the first line complements the corresponding term in the second line ('fu' / 'shou' ; sea / mountain; east / south). (continued on page 79)

壽比南山

Life as enduring as the tallest mountain

Shou Bi Nan Shan

(Longevity - comparable to - south - mountain)

The characteristics of the metaphors further enhance the concepts of 'fu' and 'shou'.

That is, one would like good fortune to be fluid, smooth, limitless like the ocean; while one would like to feel as certain of a long life as one is confident the mountains will endure. These phrases can be used individually or together, in speaking or writing.

囍 Xi

Double happiness, Marital bliss

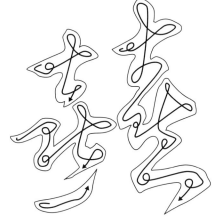

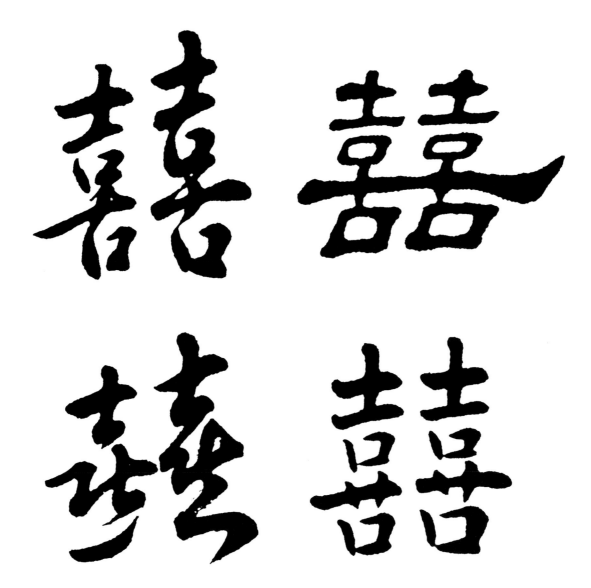

Wedding. As it appears, this is two characters joined to make one; the single character means happiness, while the two together stand for marital bliss.

This character is exclusively associated with weddings. It appears on invitations, gifts, banners, decorations, cakes and clothes, ideally in gold and red. You may find it framed and hanging throughout the year on the walls of Chinese restaurants where wedding banquets are held.

佳偶天成

Marriage blessed by heaven

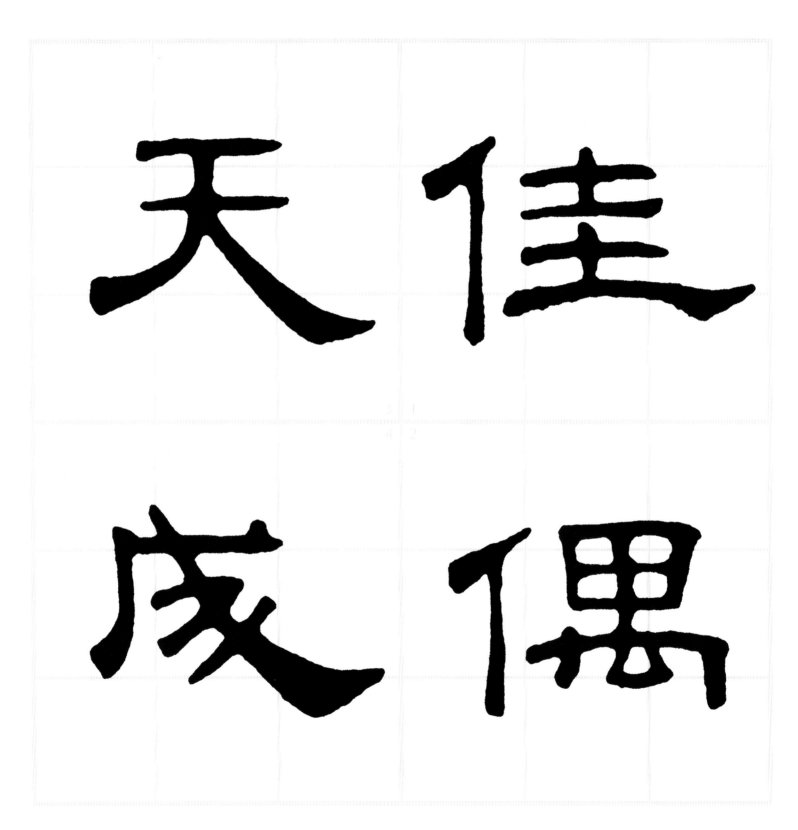

佳　佳　佳　佳
偶　偶　偶　偶
　　天　天　天
　　成　成　成

Jia Ou Tian Cheng

(fine - coincidentally - heaven - completed)

The implication of this phrase is that what began by coincidence has been sanctioned by heaven as a perfect union.

百年好合

Happy together for a hundred years

  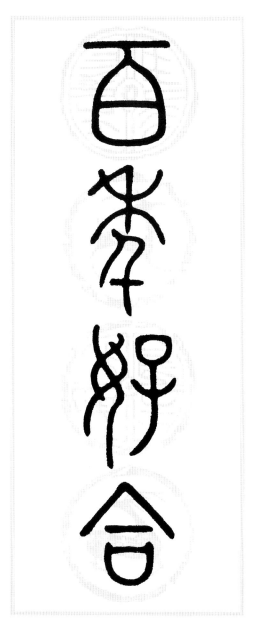

Bai Nian Hao He

(One hundred - years - good - union)

Wedding. Two-line poems are considered particularly apporopriate for weddings. Hence, the two phrases on these facing pages can be used individually, or together.

The phrase on this page has inspired a dessert that is now traditional for wedding banquets. It is a sweet soup by the same name, made of lily bulbs (known as 'bai he') and lotus root (whose name 'lian' rhymes with 'nian').

永結同心

Eternal union of two hearts

Yong Jie Tong Xin

(Eternal - knot - same, together - heart)

In this second phrase, the second character 'jie' stands for the compound 'jie hun' (結婚), meaning to marry or to conclude a marriage contract.

珠聯璧合

Pearls and Jade: Perfect complements

  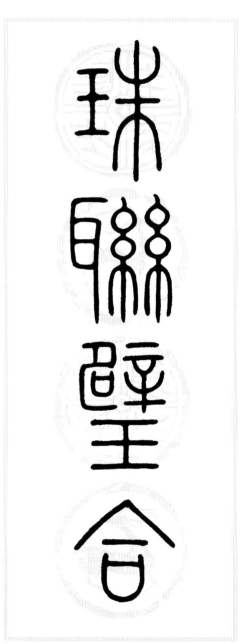

Zhu Lian Bi He

(Pearls - string - jade ring - union)

Wedding. As with the previous two phrases, the phrases on pages 86 and 87 may be used alone or together, as a couplet. The image invoked by the phrase above is of a string of pearls passing through a jade ring, becoming a single beautiful necklace, metaphor of a perfect marriage.

龍鳳呈祥

Dragon and Phoenix: Supreme union blesses all

Long Feng Cheng Xiang

(Dragon - phoenix - show - auspicious)

In this second phrase, the mythical dragon and phoenix represent, respectively, the male and female principles—or, in this context, husband and wife. The union of the two is a synergy of great power, totally in accord with universal principles; it invokes great luck and brings blessings for everyone in the community.

喜獲麟兒

Congratulations on your new son: You've captured a wondrous Qilin!

Xi Huo Lin Er

(Happy - capture - Chinese unicorn - child; son)

New baby boy. The third character here refers to the Chinese unicorn, a mythical beast famed for being lively and cute, and having magical powers. Hence, the phrase expresses congratulations and delight, as well as a hint of the challenges of raising such a spirited creature once you've caught him!

明珠入掌

Congratulations on your new daughter: A shining pearl to treasure!

Ming Zhu Ru Shou
(Bright - pearl - enters - hand)

New baby girl. The pearl is a revered symbol of purity, grace, and all that is precious in a feminine sense. The phrase suggests that a daughter is a treasure to be protected as well as appreciated.

鵬程萬里

Great ability carries you far

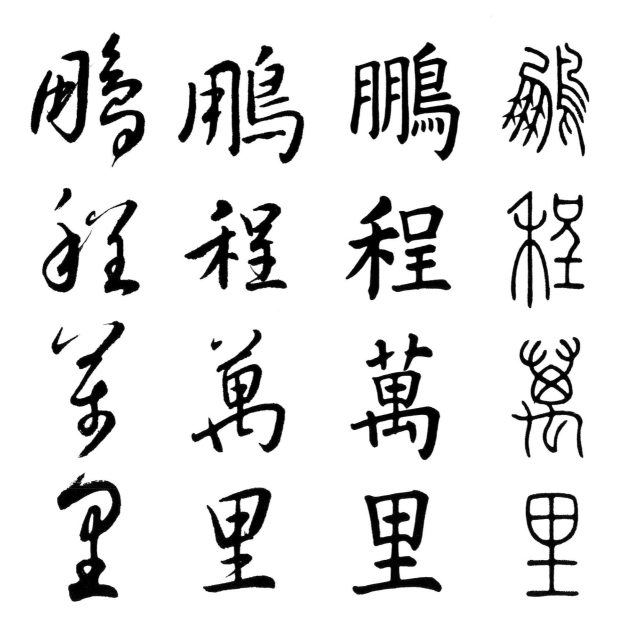

Peng Cheng Wan Li

(Mythical bird - journey - ten thousand - miles)

Graduation, New Job, New Career. The 'peng' is a huge mythical bird whose wings could carry it a thousand 'li' in an instant. Hence, this phrase describes a person whose capabilities will enable him to make great progress in his new field or career.

一帆風順

One sail, steady wind:
Smooth sailing!

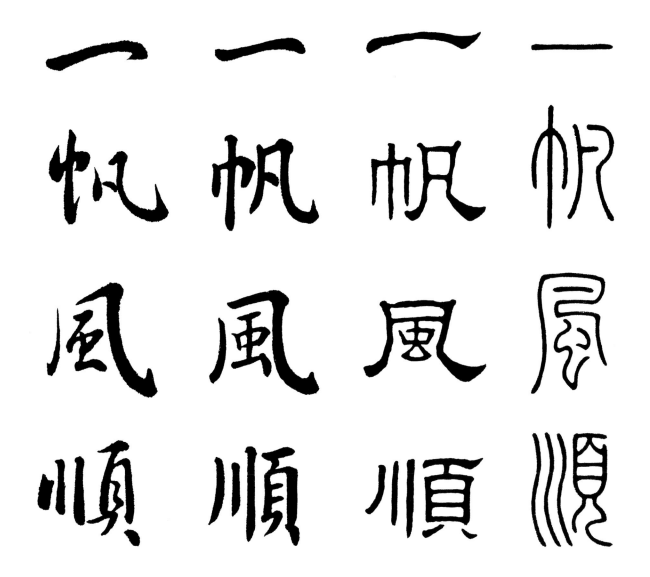

Yi Fan Feng Shun

(One - sail - wind - smooth)

Travelling. This is the seafarers' equivalent to the Irish saying, "May the road rise to meet your feet". Using only one sail, or one setting of multiple sails, means the wind is blowing in your direction; 'smooth' implies continuous, effortless, even-keeled progress. Hence, this is used to bid travelers a safe and pleasant journey, as well as to wish anyone well as they embark on a new career.

喬遷之喜
Happy moving!

Qiao Qian Zhi Xi

(Move house - of - happiness)

New House. The first two characters comprise an idiomatic compound. The phrase is used in speaking or writing.

鴻圖大展

A grand plan unfolds

Hong Tu Da Zhan

(Large - scheme, plan, project - big - unroll, unfold)

Grand Opening. The first character carries the connotations of flight, because the right side of the character is the radical for 'bird', and of waves because it is part of a compound used to describe ocean breakers. The second character brings to mind the image of a map or blueprint. Hence, the entire phrase suggests that what is at hand is a great undertaking sweeping forward as grandly as a huge bird, and coming to fruition as inexorably as waves breaking on shore.

東成西就

Success in all directions

Dong Cheng Xi Jiu

(East - complete - west - undertake)

For Success in Any Undertaking. The second and fourth words are commonly used together as a compound meaning achievement. In China as in the West, the compass points for the sun's rising and setting represent 'all directions'. This phrase appears during Chinese New Year and at other times when a new venture is underway.

早日康復

Quick recovery!

Zao Ri Kangfu

(Early - sun, day - recover from illness)

Recovery from Illness. The first two characters are a common idiom meaning "soon". 'Kang' is also the second half of the common compound 'jiankang' (see page 103) meaning "health". Hence, this is a simple, sincere wish for a return to glowing health.

身體健康

Good health!

Shen Ti Jian Kang

(Life - body - healthy - healthy)

For General Wellbeing. This is a common phrase of polite well-wishing. It is most often used as a closing for personal letters (in which case it is prefaced by the phrase, 'zhu ni', 祝你, meaning "wishing you"), but it also appears in New Year's banners and can be used as a 'get well' affirmation for anyone under the weather.

妙手回春

Exquisite skill gives a new lease on life

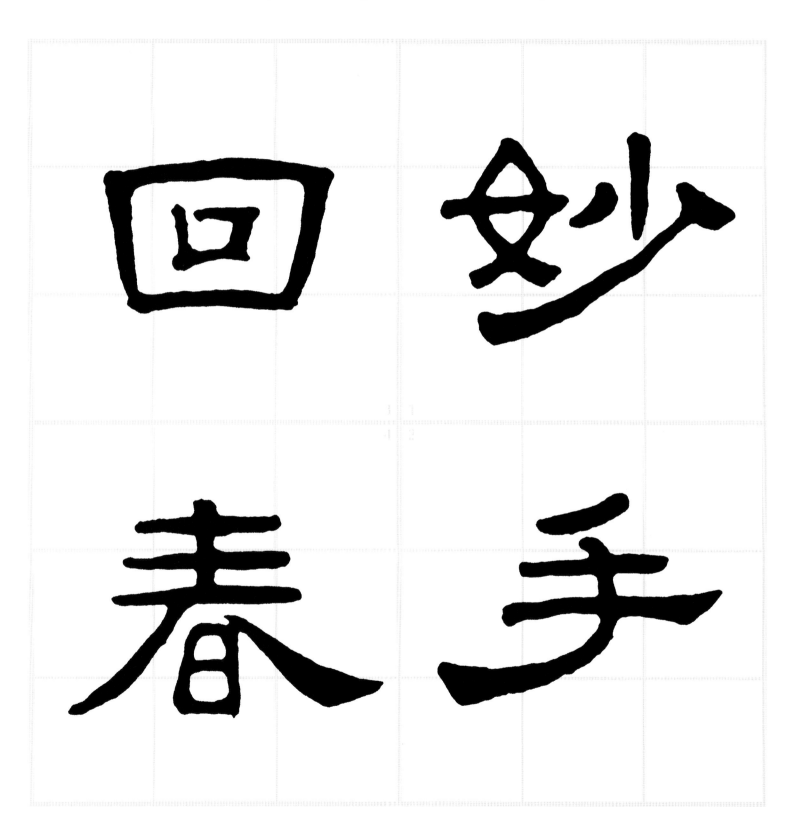

Miao Shou Hui Chun

(Wonderful - hands - return - spring)

Thanking a Doctor. This phrase is used to thank a doctor for treatment. The last character, spring, symbolizes youth, health, rejuvenation, and rebirth. Hence it is a good image for the joy that every patient feels on regaining his/her health. (On a lighter note, this phrase might also be used to thank someone who gives you a good massage, haircut, or beauty treatment.)

仁心仁術

Compassionate in heart and action

Ren Xin Ren Shu

(Benevolence - heart - benevolence - method, technique)

Thanking a Doctor. This phrase is used to thank a doctor who has shown great skill and compassion.

榮休之喜

Happy retirement!

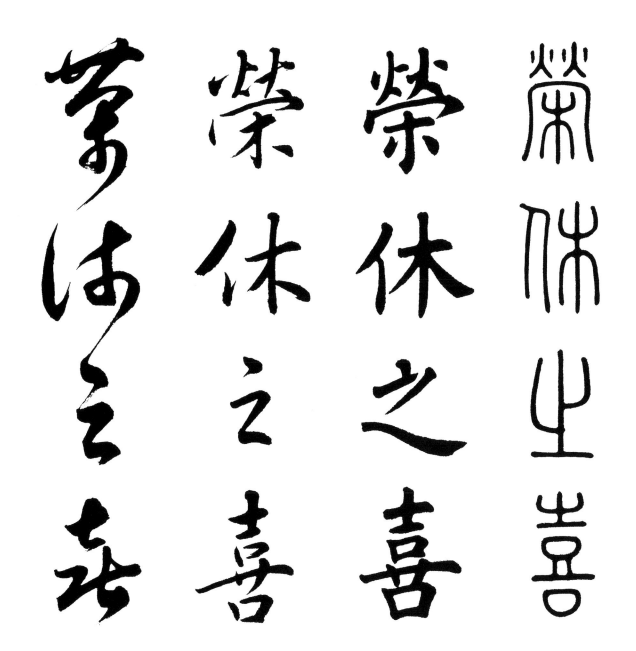

Rong Xiu Zhi Xi

(Honorable, glorious - rest, stop - of - happiness)

Retirement. Written or spoken, this phrase expresses respect for the retiree, acknowledgement of dedicated and honorable work, and wishes for well-deserved happiness in the future.

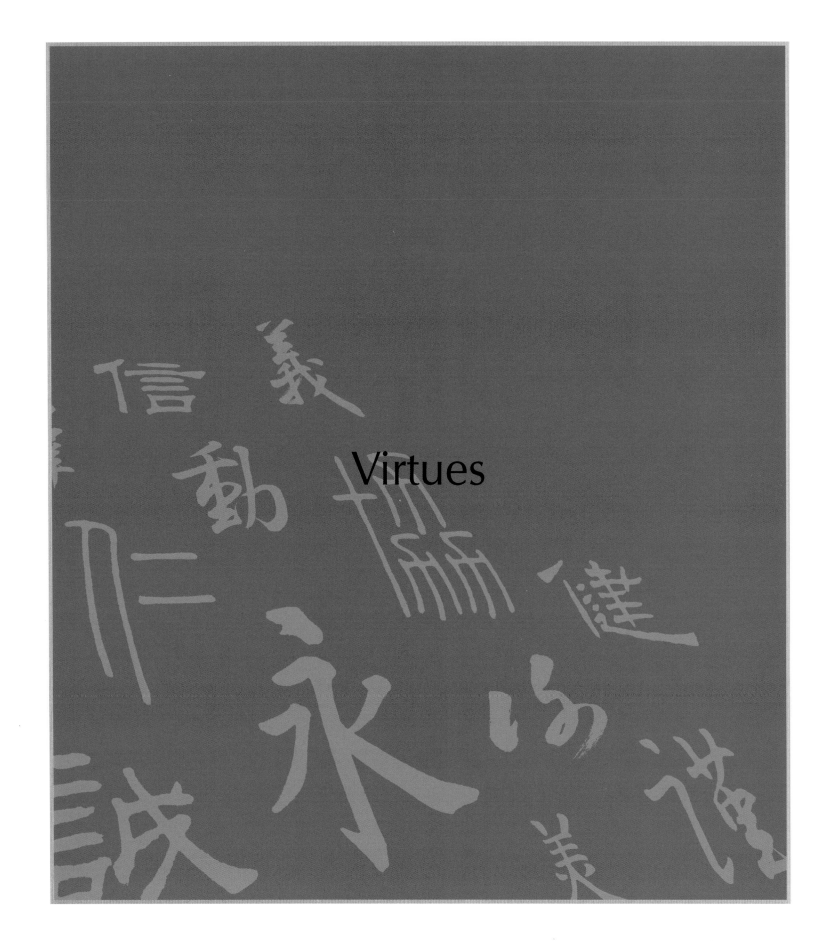

Virtues

In this section, the words are grouped according to radical (for explanation of radicals, see page 9 of the Introduction), as these fundamental components are keys to both writing and understanding the words.

All the characters in this section may be displayed as single words.

人 **Ren**

Person

仁 **Ren**
Benevolence

信 **Xin**
Trust

儉 **Jian**
Thrift

健 **Jian**
Health, vigor

心 **Xin**

Heart

愛 Ai
Love

德 De
Virtue

忍 Ren
Forbearance

忠 Zhong
Loyalty

言 Yan

Words

誠 **Cheng**

Sincere, honest and true

謙 **Qian**

Modest, humble, reserved

謹 **Jin**

Prudent, careful, respectful

謝 **Xie**

Thanks

力 **Li**
Power

勇 Yong

Courage, bravery, valor

協 Xie

To agree, to be united, cooperation

動 Dong

To move, dynamic

羊 **Yang**

Sheep

美 **Mei**

Beauty

善 **Shan**

Kindness, compassion

義 **Yi**

Justice, righteousness

Animals of
the Chinese Zodiac

Animals of the Chinese Zodiac

鼠 **Shu**
Rat

牛 **Niu**
Ox

虎 **Hu**
Tiger

兔 **Tu**
Rabbit

龍 **Long**
Dragon

蛇 **She**
Snake

馬 **Ma**
Horse

羊 **Yang**
Sheep

猴 **Hou**
Monkey

雞 **Ji**
Rooster

狗 **Gou**
Dog

豬 **Zhu**
Pig

New Year's Days of the Chinese Zodiac

The following chart gives the first day of the new year of the zodiac animal indicated.

RAT	24 Jan 1936	10 Feb 1948	28 Jan 1960	16 Jan 1972	2 Feb 1984	19 Feb 1996
OX	11 Feb 1937	29 Jan 1949	15 Feb 1961	3 Feb 1973	20 Feb 1985	8 Feb 1997
TIGER	31 Jan 1938	17 Feb 1950	5 Feb 1962	23 Jan 1974	9 Feb 1986	28 Jan 1998
RABBIT	19 Feb 1939	6 Feb 1951	25 Jan 1963	11 Feb 1975	29 Jan 1987	16 Feb 1999
DRAGON	8 Feb 1940	27 Jan 1952	13 Feb 1964	31 Jan 1976	17 Feb 1988	5 Feb 2000
SNAKE	27 Jan 1941	14 Feb 1953	2 Feb 1965	18 Feb 1977	6 Feb 1989	24 Jan 2001
HORSE	15 Feb 1942	3 Feb 1954	21 Jan 1966	7 Feb 1978	27 Jan 1990	12 Feb 2002
SHEEP	5 Feb 1943	24 Jan 1955	9 Feb 1967	28 Jan 1979	15 Feb 1991	1 Feb 2003
MONKEY	25 Jan 1944	12 Feb 1956	30 Jan 1968	16 Feb 1980	4 Feb 1992	22 Jan 2004
ROOSTER	13 Feb 1945	31 Jan 1957	17 Feb 1969	5 Feb 1981	23 Jan 1993	9 Feb 2005
DOG	2 Feb 1946	18 Feb 1958	6 Feb 1970	25 Jan 1982	10 Feb 1994	29 Jan 2006
PIG	22 Jan 1947	8 Feb 1959	27 Jan 1971	13 Feb 1983	31 Jan 1995	18 Feb 2007

Templates

In this section you will find patterns and templates to aid both practice and production.

The first template is a simple grid, like the practice paper used by Chinese students in learning to write. Photocopy this, then use it underneath paper which you can see through; when compared with the large characters written on similar grids earlier in the book, the lines should help you get the shape and proportions of the characters correct.

Following the grid are templates for the Good Fortune character (typically a diamond) and Double Happiness (typically a circle), while the last two templates (one contemprary, one traditional) are rectangular patterns suitable for displaying any of the four–character phrases.

We suggest you photocopy these outlines first onto plain paper for practicing, and finally onto decorative paper for making cards and posters.

Happy writing!

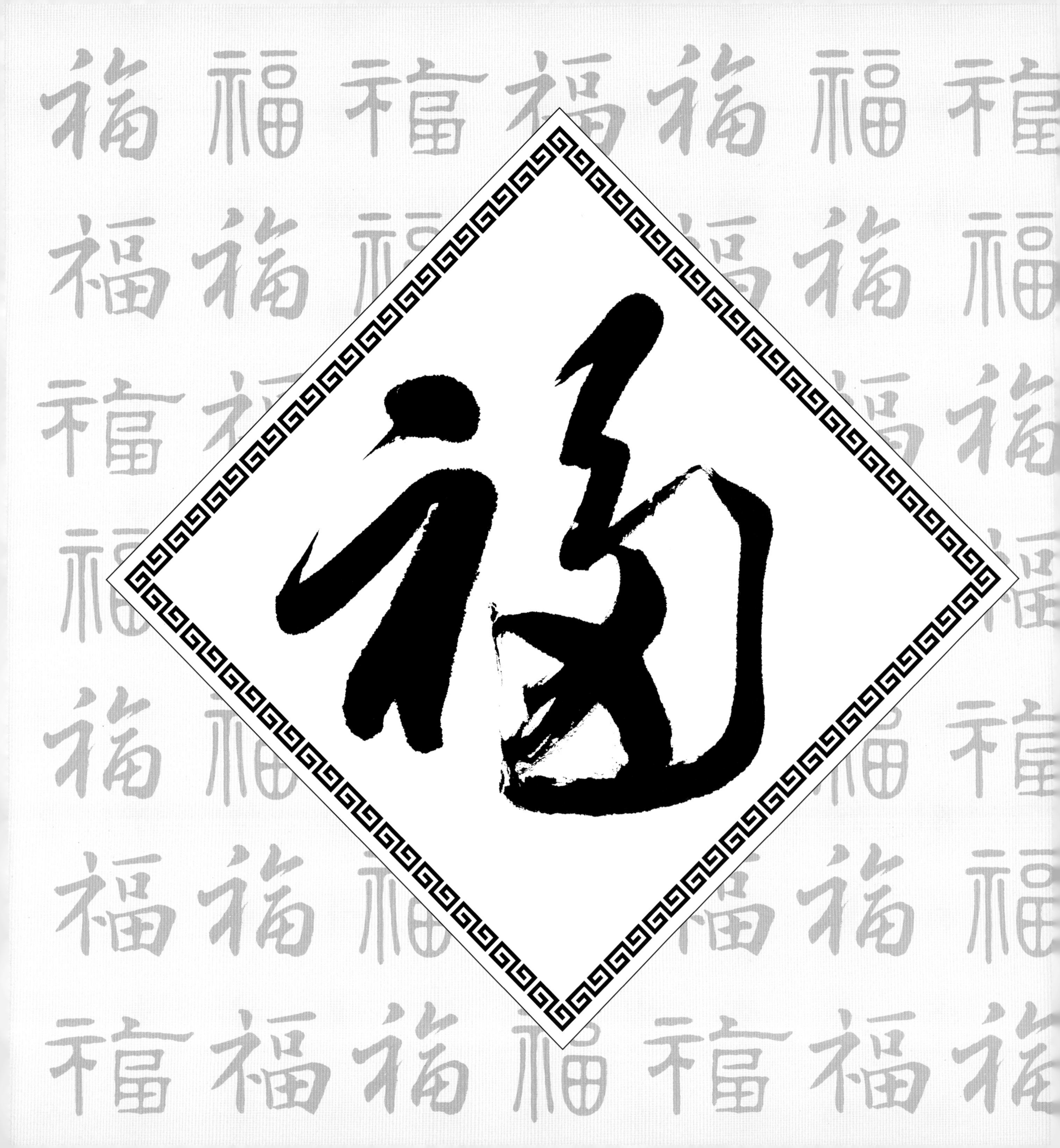
福

新年快樂

大吉大利

福如東海
壽比南山

INDEX TO PINYIN PRONUNCIATIONS

INDEX TO ENGLISH TRANSLATIONS

141